WHAT OTHERS ARE SAYING

I have known Randy for almost 20 years. We met when he was a client of the bank I worked for at the time. I was in the commercial loan department and had the responsibility of building additional business relationships with our clients. After speaking with Randy, he told me that when he was ready to move forward on a few projects, he would reach out to me.

A few years passed and I left that bank and began work at the Bank of Oklahoma as a Private Banker. One day, I got a call from Randy about building a new office building – which was new considering his firm had always rented in the past. Knowing Randy long enough, I knew that he had completed all his due diligence and was ready to get started.

After reviewing his plan, we loaned him the funds to build the new office. His business sense was evident, when business was good he accelerated his payments – often saying, "I don't like paying interest." We often joked that he was a great investment, but a terrible customer because he paid his loans off so quickly that the bank didn't have a chance to make any money off of him.

Anyone who is considering going into business for themselves should not only read this book, but live it. In addition, if an experienced entrepreneur is stumbling, this book can put them back on their feet. Randy is a straight shooter who tells things as they are. This no non-sense approach is evident in *The Entrepreneur's Roadmap to Success*.

The way that Randy takes the reader from "square one" thru inception, implementation and execution will provide the reader with guidance and a knowledge base that will help them to succeed.

His positive attitude toward business and life are contagious. As long as I have known Randy, he has never hesitated to be a mentor for others. His book will be one the business owner will want to keep handy and read time and again.

—W. Shane Garrow
Senior Vice President
The Private Bank at Bank of Oklahoma

The expertise required to build and achieve scalable and transferable business success is a skill possessed by few individuals.

The Entrepreneur's Roadmap to Success is a real life compendium of valuable business knowledge that provides direction and insight to the reader.

This book provides candidly honest opinions and insightful questions to consider while weighing if the challenging path of an entrepreneur is the right direction to take for the reader. The author brings his experiences to bear on the hard-hitting emotional self-examination that will be encountered by the reader if they have the courage to take on the challenge of entrepreneurialism.

I became acquainted with Randy in the final 1/3 of his career when he became affiliated with my firm and continued to build a successful Financial Services firm which consistently ranked in the top 2% of my firm.

Randy's vision, planning, and process for building his business was a topic he routinely shared with me over the life of our business relationship and friendship. Randy executed his written plans in a way that set him apart from those who planned but never executed. In my opinion, Randy's due diligence and the discipline he exhibited in his pro forma are two of the critical pieces that ultimately fueled the exponential growth of his firm.

Over the years, Randy has provided his expertise and counsel to the financial representatives of our firm at several different events. His passion for providing excellent service to his clients is evident in the energy and enthusiasm he exhibited building a strong practice that focused on caring for his client's best interests. I have personally encouraged Randy to seek speaking engagements at agency and wholesaler meetings or in any group setting where he can offer his in-person expertise and training to budding entrepreneurs.

Anyone looking to starting down the avenue of starting a business, as well as those looking to improve their current business position would benefit from the consolidation of sound advice offered in *The Entrepreneur's Roadmap to Success*.

—Todd Kinart
President/CEO
SII Investments Inc.

DEDICATION

I want to thank God for giving me the energy to work hard and do what I needed to do in life, and for the many blessings in my life and family.

I am thankful for my wife who taught me to care and to believe in others.

Special thanks also to my dad and mother who taught me to not only have a good work ethic but convinced me through a positive attitude that I could do anything I set my mind to do.

I am thankful for my children, for who they are and for the sacrifices they have made in life.

Lastly, I am thankful for my grandchildren, for they give me hope for a better future.

FOREWORD

Randy Steele has decades of experience and great business acumen. An aspiring entrepreneur will find this handbook of great value and comfort. It will suggest roads to travel and the pitfalls to avoid. It will provide cautious encouragement of the rewards and sacrifices required of a successful business owner.

Tried and tested. The author shares his treasure trove of experience to inspire both the rookie business dreamer and the seasoned entrepreneur to develop into a successful businessperson.

Simply stated, it cleverly explains the fundamental workings of the key business enterprise components... from management to finance, marketing to accounting, and even touching on the legal ramifications of owning a business. This book is a one-stop source to guide an entrepreneur down the path to success. Through simple storytelling, the reader will gain great insight and navigation skills from a person who has traveled numerous business avenues, from idea to implementation.

This book is not a work of fiction. It is not about a character. It is about everyday small business issues and how to approach reasonable and workable solutions. I have personally used several of the author's ideas and strategies in my own practice over the years. I hold him in high regard as both a friend and as someone whom I have worked with on numerous occasions.

The stories he discusses will enhance the entrepreneur's vision as to what to watch out for and ways to avoid cataclysmic mistakes. You will certainly read this book over and over again as it becomes your Roadmap to Success.

—Jeff Rhodes, Attorney, Riseling & Rhodes

CONTENTS

INTRODUCTION

Since my start as a businessman almost 40 years ago, I have watched so many things change. In the past, our marketplace was the town where we hung our shingle. And maybe if we were lucky, we could also help other customers or clients in towns that were not too far away.

Today, thanks to technology, our world is much smaller, so much so that we view our marketplace as the entire world. Even though we may take care of and/or service customers and clients in a smaller geographic area, we regularly buy goods and services globally. Technology, the internet, shipping methods, travel, and more have changed the way we think and how we do business.

That makes creating a perfect business blueprint, detailed with all the right features, moves, options, and ideas, a complete impossibility. It's not going to happen! There is no way to get every single setting just right to meet every single niche need and opportunity out there.

So take the pressure off yourself to be perfect before you launch, or to be perfect within 12 months, or to do everything perfectly as you grow your business.

Things grow and change, and part of being in business is learning to flow and adapt. It makes you better, and it also opens up new opportunities that may not have existed just a few short weeks ago!

With that said, we must build a plan that can be modified as we learn from our own experiences, from the experiences of others, and from the ever-changing world around us.

I need to warn you that being in business for yourself is not for sissies! However, it will be the most fulfilling job you will ever have, and if done correctly you can either build a legacy that can be passed on to future generations or a business that will have value and attract other entrepreneurs.

One great thing about the business world is that you don't have to make your decision today. You can decide as you go if the legacy route (for your future family) or the entrepreneur route (for other businesspeople who want to buy you out) is better for you. There is no pressure to make that decision right now. You have the time to make up your mind which way is best for you.

The purpose of this book is not to identify each and every situation that you will encounter in your business. There is no way anyone can do that. But there are enough similar principles that should help you analyze your own business and will help you make the best possible choices.

My hope is that this book will give you some "down to earth" insights on how to set up and build a successful business or practice that will be of value to you as an entrepreneur. If you are already in business, there are plenty of ideas and techniques that will be helpful along the way.

The opinions I have are mine, but I share them with you based on years of experience in the business world. To be sure, there are many ways you can set up and run a successful business. I am confident, however, that if you follow the guidelines that I outline in these pages, you *will be* successful!

I'm not bragging or trying to deceive you in any way. I'm telling you the truth. I've been there and done that, and in these pages I'm putting it all on the table for you to study and benefit from. It's yours, if you want it.

Enjoy!

—Randy R. Steele

CHAPTER ONE

YOUR INITIAL CHALLENGE

Business requires clear thinking, but having a clear head to consider a business idea or opportunity is often a lot more difficult than it seems. This is the direct result of the many factors that naturally influence our decision making.

Careful evaluation requires honesty — complete unashamed honesty. Do we view owning our own business as a way to escape our own little world? Are we making decisions based on fear? Or desire for comfort? Or out of greed? Or out of competition?

There are so many scenarios and powerful pressures that affect us, be they health, family, or financial. You name it, we face limitless pressures, and it is *extremely* hard to make an informed decision when under pressure.

With so many unknowns swirling around, I will say this:

One true motivation for success in business is to make sure you are moving toward something better, not running from something unpleasant.

Small Steps First

At first, begin by taking only simple or small steps in the right direction. Yes, well-meaning family members and friends will encourage you to "go for it," but what they really should be advising is the importance of making sure you have done your homework ("due diligence" in business terms).

I recognize that most of us do not want to think about, or much less be told to do our "due diligence," but this is what I have found:

> *Your business idea has almost 100% chance of failing if you do not do your due diligence.*

What's more, if you don't truly understand the features and mechanics of the business you are considering, there is no way you can even do proper due diligence. That is a serious thought worth pondering before you get too far down the road with your mental projections.

Along those lines, a friend of mine once told me, "You never get paid for more than you do, until you do more than you get paid for." Another way of saying that, as it relates to your new business, is to say:

> *You will never get more out of your business than what you put into it.*

Looking at the Little Things

Many people will jump into business without thinking too much about the little things. Does the business venture even make sense? How much do they know about the industry? Is there even a demand for their product or services?

Important questions … left unanswered! But you must answer those questions, and many more, if you are going to be successful.

I can't tell you how many uninformed reasons I have heard over the years as to why someone wanted to go into business. Statements like, "I think I'll start a restaurant because I really like to cook" or "I am thinking about opening a fishing guide service because I really like to fish, and I'm good at it."

The bottom line is they do not have a clue on how to start, much less run, a successful business. Starting, running, and staying in business are not easy tasks! If you are already in business, you know exactly what I am talking about. It takes someone with a strong personality who doesn't take "no" or "it won't work" for an answer, and who always looks for ways to make things happen.

One not so little thing is communication. Successful business leaders are communicators, and they know or learn the terminology of their industry. Sometimes we may drop the ball, but we must be constant, active communicators.

Many years ago, I was visiting with a potential client and making small talk. The woman was saying how mad her husband got with her for buying so many CDs. She had bought three the week before and had bought ten that month.

I was thinking, "Is her husband an idiot? Why would he complain about someone saving money with that frequency?" I didn't know how much money was put into each CD or if her CDs were going for college planning, retirement or just savings, but I was on her side.

Then her husband muttered, "We don't have the money to waste on music!"

Oops! I thought they were talking about CDs as in Certificates of Deposit, not CDs as in Compact Discs of music. I was going down the wrong path, but I quickly changed gears and sided with the husband.

As the business leader, make sure from the beginning of the conversation that you are talking the same language as your client.

Step #1: Find a Need and Fill It

To have a successful business, you **must** "find a need and fill it." This is paramount. You cannot ignore this, for this is the central reason for the very existence of your business.

You may have heard the "find a need and fill it" phrase before, but I take that one step further and say that if you want to have a truly rewarding business, then you need to "find the hurt and help heal it."

Quite often, the need is overshadowed by a hurt that is affecting the person, and once the hurt starts healing, the need often changes.

By combining these two concepts together, identifying the need and the hurt, you have elevated your business to the status of being an **extraordinary** business.

Your entire focus is on your customers and clients and you truly have their best interests in mind. You can't go wrong with that, and it is a relationship that will last a lifetime.

The formula looks something like this:

1) Find a need and fill it

+

2) Find the hurt and help heal it

=

3) Extraordinary business!

When we look at the needs of our clients, we see that their needs come in all different shapes and sizes. Many times the real need is disguised as something else, so it is hard to really see what the true need is.

If you have little children or grandchildren, you know that when they are fussing the immediate need is to figure out what is wrong. Are they hungry, do they want to be held, or maybe they have a dirty diaper? Similarly, in business, your clients will have different needs. The better you get at meeting those needs, the more successful your business will be.

Step #2: Know That Change Is Inevitable

In business it is vital that you know, and always keep in mind, that change is inevitable. What worked yesterday may or may not work today or tomorrow. Everything changes, and that doesn't mean it always changes for the good either!

Technology is one of those things that is usually a change for the better, but things are constantly changing around us, from trash bags to plastics to glass products to vehicles we drive to food we eat. Everything is trying to improve, and we see it in the constant striving for stronger, longer-lasting, and safer products.

Change is constant, and if you can be aware and also *use* that reality to your advantage, all the better.

Step #3: Understand the Need

Your business meets a need, but is that need short-term in nature or is it long-term with repeat purchases? This must honestly and carefully be figured out because things can go well or go terribly wrong if the type of need you are trying to fill is misunderstood. Along those lines, you must also clarify if the need is one that the same consumer will need continually.

Another consideration in identifying your business need is to make sure your idea is legal. Now, before you go crazy on me, I am not suggesting you pursue an illegal business, but do you know if your business idea will be impacted by the rules and regulations in the counties, cities, and states where you want to operate? One single rule or regulation could make your grand idea no longer feasible.

I have seen zoning restrictions, licensing issues, and even hours of operation put a big damper on great business ideas. One friend purchased a building in the downtown area of his city. It was the perfect location for his new business; it included plenty of parking and was ideal in every respect ... except that the building was on the historical register, which meant that some of the modifications he needed to make to his building were not allowed.

To say the least, he was not a happy camper, but if he had only done his research completely, this type of situation could have probably been avoided.

Imagine setting up a bait shop on an old fishing pier that no longer allowed fishing! You wouldn't want to do that, would you? So spend the time you need to really evaluate your idea before you get too far down the road.

Understand the Need

When I travel around the country training and meeting with businessmen, when the conversation moves over to insurance, the walls start going up. One common objection I hear is, "I don't believe in insurance." It's time to understand the need!

I ask them to clarify what they mean. Are they saying they don't believe in insurance or that they don't want to pay for insurance? As you would expect, they chuckle and 99% of them will say, "Well, I don't like throwing my money away on insurance."

Further clarification and understanding is needed! I then explain that they don't need to insure everything, just any of those items or persons they can't afford to lose. I go on to explain that by transferring the risk to someone else (the insurance company) they will be able to continue to operate their company as before, just with less risk or pressure.

I point out that if they are going to be both a successful and wise businessman, they have to understand the concept of transferring risk to someone else and the benefits that come with it. Choosing to "self-insure" comes with risks they may not like.

At this point, I start seeing the "deer in the headlight" look and they nod their heads and say they have never thought about it this way.

Then, to drive my point home, I ask them what their greatest asset is and they all say that they are their own greatest asset.

Now, when all their walls are down, I bluntly ask them, "Then please tell me why a wise businessman does not insure his greatest asset?"

At that point, there is usually not a lot more to discuss. They now understand the need and there is nothing left to do, except finish the paperwork.

Sometimes I'll need to explain the different types of insurances, beyond health and liability, that are most commonly forgotten, such as (E&O) errors & omission insurance, (DI) disability insurance, and (BOE) business overhead insurance.

They have not thought through these questions:

- How would your company make it if you were to become disabled?
- What if you were sued?
- Do you have the time and resources to handle the distraction?
- If you have business partners and one of the partners dies, do you want to be in business with the deceased partner's spouse?

Having an insurance professional help with these decisions is really important, and by gaining additional knowledge and education, you are simply reducing your risks.

Is There Money In It?

The biggest question that your business idea must answer is whether there is really any money in your proposal. I mean, you see the need and you are looking to meet that need, but is this idea financially feasible?

Even if you can afford to throw money at your idea, you must be able to answer:

> Will this idea sustain itself through good times and bad? Is this idea truly financially sound?

That is a big question, one that many people will avoid answering. You cannot. Every successful business has figured out a way to make money.

Sounds like common sense, but you would be surprised!

Dig a little deeper and ask yourself:

> *Will I be able to pay the bills with this business in the future if the market changes or the economy weakens?*

For instance, let's say you have a boat rental business in a tourist area. Business is going great in the usual economy, but would customers continue to come if there was an economic downturn? And if there was a downturn and you aren't renting very many boats, would you make it? Do you have enough staying power? Have you diversified your product mix to meet with good times and not-so-good times?

One example of this "diversified mix" would be a lawn mowing business in the spring/summer that becomes a tree trimming and snow removal business in the fall/winter. These two businesses would work well together and complement each other. How can your business do that?

Clearly, the bottom line is the success of your business, which means looking for ways to diversify ... so that you make sure your business stays healthy!

More Preparation Is Better

The more you prepare, the better you and your business will be. That takes time and effort, but it is worth every second you spend.

Admittedly, you have a lot to think about and consider, but it is one of the necessary details that you must struggle through if you are going to turn your idea into a successful business venture.

Yes, you will need to make decisions that are uncomfortable, unpleasant, or unpopular. It's tempting to procrastinate and put off the decisions that really need to be made now, but don't do it! Here is the truth:

> *Business leaders are leaders because they make those necessary, yet tough, decisions.*

Each day when I get up, I make a "to-do" list of tasks that I would like to get accomplished. I'm sure most of you do the same thing or something similar. Some of the tasks are ones that I can do in a very short amount of time, like taking out the trash, to ones that take much longer, like cleaning the garage. Some items get carried over from yesterday's list, or even last week's list.

We all have our own system, but here is a universal truth for all of us who make "to-do" lists:

Scratching a task off our list is incredibly satisfying!

Apply that same desire to feel good, to feel that sense of completion, to all your tasks, even the tasks that you don't really want to attack. Leave no room for procrastination.

This will serve you well as you dive deeper into your business idea.

Take Action Now

Pause for a minute.

1. Write down on a piece of paper (or on the Note Pages in the back of this book) your business idea.
2. Then go through the analysis we just discussed and see if any of your ideas pass the "smell test."
3. After you have gone through this exercise, and you feel you have analyzed your need-based business idea, then the next step is to start putting your numbers together.

CHAPTER TWO

Talking About Your Numbers

The numbers ... it all starts with the numbers. When you are starting a business, you will find that the numbers have a way of reducing everything to the bottom line:

Your costs vs. your profits.

When you start putting the numbers together, you will be amazed to see how much things cost! The dream of somehow going into business for a "little-or-nothing" investment is really just that ... a dream! Guess what? You can't do it.

Many basic expenses, such as taxes, maintenance fees, and insurance are often overlooked when new business owners initially crunch their numbers. As a result, the businesses end up struggling when they really didn't need to, had they reviewed all their numbers.

My advice to you:

Go over your numbers again and again. Then wait a couple of days or even a week and go over them again.

Doing multiple reviews of your numbers is part of your necessary preparation, and spacing it out over a few days or a week allows your brain to work when it is more relaxed. You may be surprised what you will find!

Think Into the Future

To make sure you are on the right track, it is always a good idea to do at least a 2-year **pro forma** analysis. In the investing world, a pro forma report is a:

> "Projected or estimated financial statement that attempts to present a reasonably accurate idea of what a firm's financial situation would be if the present trends continue or certain assumptions hold true."

Pro forma statements are routinely used in preparing "what if" scenarios, creating your business plans, estimating possible cash requirements, or when submitting financing proposals to those who need to see them.

In my opinion, creating a 3-year or even a 4-year pro forma analysis would be a good idea. Granted, the "numbers" in the first two years of this analysis will have more validity than the last two years, but the thought process you go through to arrive at these numbers is also important as a learning tool.

The numbers of your estimated financial situation a few years into the future will prove to be far better, and far more accurate, than any "hope and pray we make it" approach that some try to use when they are starting their business. Trust me, and trust your numbers!

If You Are Getting Investment Capital

If you are going to try to get financing, most banks will require at least a 2-year pro forma statement. So stick with your numbers and generate your pro forma.

Years ago, I asked a banker friend why most banks required at least a 2-year statement. He insightfully said, "The main reason we require at least a 2-year pro forma is to see if the customer has enough vision to see themselves still in business in two years."

Wow, that is good logic! I thought that was really pretty insightful but also pretty alarming, for no doubt that is based on experience.

Here is a truth that always applies, especially at this point where financing is involved:

> *Make sure you plan, prepare, and then execute your plan.*

To make sure your pro forma report is done properly you will need to hire an accountant or an accounting firm to put your numbers together. They will not only develop a presentation for you but also a presentation in the format for your bank and any other potential investors.

Incidentally, you want to make sure that whoever puts together your report uses the generally accepted accounting principles format (GAAP). Most likely your accountant will do just that.

Also, as a side note, when you are choosing a banker and banking firm to partner with, do your due diligence and check them out. Make sure they are right for you.

When I was looking at changing banks and bankers, I would use a little test. Since I enjoyed golf, I would ask a new potential banker if he played golf. If he did, I would invite him to a friendly round of golf. I would say, "Whoever loses the round buys dinner and drinks."

One prospective banker, in our "friendly round of golf," would almost always kick the ball to a better position for a shot. It wasn't a big deal, but it was still not right. It showed me what type of person I would be working with if I went with him and his bank. I felt that if he would act this way here, then there was no telling what he would do in the business world where greater pressure and greater profits were sure to be on the table.

Maybe it was silly on my part to feel this way and to weed out potential bankers based on how they acted when they played a round of golf, but of the times I chose not to go with certain bankers, many of those bankers were not with their banks very long. They quit, moved on, or were fired. Perhaps it was coincidental, but it seemed to work for me.

Keep Track of the Numbers

In my opinion, being smart enough to run your own business also means that you are smart enough to run the numbers yourself or to hire a CPA to run them for you. We will soon discuss CPAs in more detail, but my point here is that you must have a system in place to track your numbers.

As you start looking at your numbers and begin the business process, always build extra funds into your plan. Always!

How Much Funding Is Enough?

I suggest that you borrow enough for you to maintain your current lifestyle at home for one full year. You will be spending more time working on your business during your first year than you can imagine right now, so it's best to have enough money on hand so that you don't have to worry about paying the bills at home.

Any good financial institution will understand that. And if they don't, go somewhere else. When it comes to funding, never forget this important truth:

> *It is vital that you are not undercapitalized when you begin operations.*

Many businesses don't make it because they do not have enough working capital when they start out. And you must, at all times, preserve your working capital, for your working capital is the life-blood of your company.

In my first business, I did all the things we have discussed here ... except one thing. I did not have enough of a cushion to handle the unexpected expenses. That meant I was undercapitalized right out of the gates!

This became immediately apparent when I started buying the items I needed, only to find one item cost a few dollars more and another cost several hundred dollars more than I had budgeted. I thought my budget was great, but I had nothing built in to handle the unexpected.

To make things worse, since I was already under construction, unforeseen items such as additional electrical or plumbing work simply had to be done. I couldn't stop, much less object, even if it wasn't in my budget. If you have ever built a home or commercial building, you know exactly what I am talking about:

> *It's those necessary additional items that can really blow your budget out of the water!*

I was having a hard time making adjustments to my budget and expenditures. I spent more of my very precious working capital than I should have and honestly thought I was going out of business before I really got into business. Thankfully, my wife helped me come up with solutions to my ignorance before my mistake became lethal! I found out the hard way:

> *Preserve your working capital.*

Handling Expectations

How much things will cost and how much you will make are all parts of your plan, your budget, and your expectations, but here is something you must know:

> *Things will cost you more than you think … and you will not net as much as you think.*

If this bothers you, then maybe you are not cut out to be in business for yourself. Vince Lombardi used to say:

> "The price of success is hard work, dedication to the job at hand, and determination that

whether we win or lose, we have applied the best of ourselves to the task at hand."

To be clear, success is a product of knowledge and experience, not luck. When I hear people say "that person is just so lucky," I know that they are clueless. They have no idea what they are talking about.

What would have been better to say is, "Man, they must have really worked their butts off." That's more realistic! In fact …

The harder you work, the luckier you will be!

Handling expectations, both your own as well as those of your clients and customers, is one of those constant details that you must always work on. That involves clear communication, humility, and boldness.

Do not assume all is well. I remember, many years ago, watching the *Odd Couple* on TV and hearing one of the characters say, "To assume is to make an ass out of *u* and *me*."

What's more, you cannot assume what worked yesterday will work today or tomorrow. Things change, and a small part of properly handling expectations is being aware of the change and using it to your advantage.

Not easy, but you can handle it!

CHAPTER THREE

CHOOSING YOUR BUSINESS TYPE

You have come this far. Now it's time to talk about what type of business entity you should set up. Is your business going to be an LLC, a Sub Chapter S corporation, a Limited Partnership, Sole Proprietorship, or a C corporation?

Without diving deep into the intricacies of each business entity, it is important to know that each entity offers some of the same benefits as well as some different benefits that are only specific to that entity. What you want is the business entity that serves you best.

Work Out the Details with a CPA

As I mentioned before, having a good CPA can save you a lot of money, heartache, and time ... and this is definitely one of those times.

Before your initial meeting with your CPA to select a business entity, do familiarize yourself with the types of entities before you meet. That will make your meeting much more valuable.

You want your company to be set up to take advantage of tax-wise planning. In this ever-changing tax code world we live in, a good CPA can save you more in taxes than you will ever know! That is one of the most compelling reasons to have a CPA involved in the process.

In fact, years from now, your CPA may even recommend you change from one business entity to another. This change might be for tax reasons, reporting requirements, money savings, or ease of operations. Be open to the idea, but make sure you understand the ramifications of the proposed changes. Your CPA should have your best interests in mind, but this is **your** business and the "buck" always stops with you!

Do you know what states you plan to do business in? Make sure your CPA is aware of where you plan to operate, as some states are "community property states" and others are not. Again, familiarize yourself and understand what the differences are because it will be most helpful when you are planning.

Check Out Your CPA
When you look at CPAs, trying to find the right one for you, keep your eye open to find out what their area of specialty might be.

- Are they really a tax person or are they more like a bookkeeper? (There's nothing wrong with a bookkeeper, but that's not what you need right now.)
- Is the CPA an expert in a specific industry, such as oil, sports, gaming, nonprofits, or something else?
- Does the CPA focus on new business startups only? Or new business startups within a particular industry?
- Or maybe the CPA focuses on high-net-worth individuals with estate issues?
- Is the CPA you have chosen licensed in the states you plan to do business in?

There are countless specialties and areas of interest, so take some time to check out several CPAs. You are not offending them by "kicking the tires," so to speak, and it will be to your benefit in the end.

Quite often, a CPA is also an attorney. That doesn't mean you get two for the price of one, or that the attorney CPA is necessarily smarter. I personally like having a CPA who also has a law degree, even if the CPA doesn't practice the law. I guess I have convinced myself that the CPA is bringing more knowledge and experience to the table, but either way, the CPA must have the skills to meet your needs. Also, what about asking other business leaders in your same business for a CPA referral?

With CPAs, I swear by this principle:

> *Use CPAs who know their stuff ... because it will save you big bucks in the end!*

It will be tempting to find the most inexpensive CPA or to use a CPA who does not specialize in what you need ... but you don't go to a podiatrist when you really need a cardiologist, even though they are both doctors, do you?

I know that sounds ridiculous, but over and over again I have seen situations in business where someone was trying to cut corners and didn't get the proper advice, and it really cost them in the long run. Do not fall for this type of thinking. Trust me!

My attorney CPA used to tell me all the time, "Make sure you don't pierce the corporate veil." He would then explain to me how important it is to always keep personal funds separate from business funds. (With some types of corporations, there are rules that prohibit commingling of funds.) If you do mix the funds, your personal funds and liability become company funds and liability, and company funds and liability become your personal funds and liability!

That advice alone is worth every penny you would pay your CPA! Many business owners have created tremendous problems for themselves, their families, and their businesses because they didn't know their business entity's rules about keeping business and personals funds separate. Small detail, huge issue!

Another good reason for having a quality CPA is simply peace of mind and confidence that your personal and business financial/tax affairs are being handled properly and most efficiently. That allows you to concentrate on building your business.

Regarding CPAs:

> *Don't cut corners. Find a good CPA who meets your specific needs.*

Bring in the Attorney

Once you have determined which entity you will be using, then it is time to engage an attorney to actually set up your business entity.

Do yourself a favor and don't try to set this entity up on your own. There are a lot of online "business kits" that promise speed, ease, and low price ... but you get what you pay for. I have seen too many business leaders start down the wrong path, make unnecessary errors, or fail their necessary compliance requirements, all because they tried to do it themselves.

I'm not saying you can't do it, I'm just warning you not to. Okay, I'm begging you not to, but it's up to you.

An attorney is someone you are going need on your team, so start building that relationship from day one.

Build Your Team Right

To make sure you find the right fit for you, be it personality, expertise, pricing model, or accessibility, don't be afraid to interview several CPAs and attorneys. In truth, they are really applying for a job with you, so find a good fit.

When meeting with the CPA (tax advisor) and attorney (legal advisor), make sure you ask a lot of questions. You need to fully understand the ramifications of your decisions. Take your spouse or business partner(s) with you if you can.

I also think it is a good idea to meet with both advisors together at least once a year so that everyone is on the same page. I have had great success doing meetings this way.

Try one and see if it also works for you.

On Your Way

After you have chosen your desired business entity, you've filled out the necessary forms, and your state has approved your business and your business name, you are on your way!

CHAPTER FOUR

RIDING THE HIGHS AND LOWS

In business, just as in life, there are peaks and valleys, highs and lows, and ups and downs. Some days you'll feel like you can take on the world and other days you'll wonder if you should pull the plug.

If you are going to be in business for yourself, know that the peaks and valleys are a natural part of the process. I have found that expecting this up/down swell of emotions and challenges helps you better cope with them when they come.

Sure, the ride up is pretty breathtaking … but so is the ride down! It comes with the territory, so relax and go with the flow.

Manage the Doubts

You are going to have those days when you think you can't take it any longer and you are ready to quit. You will. Don't fret or worry, just be ready for it.

However, in that moment, things can really go from bad to worse if you start doubting all of your decisions. Doubt naturally makes you self-examine, and before you know it you'll be wondering:

- "Why did I ever start a business?"
- "Am I crazy?"
- "Will I make it?"

You have to quarantine those types of questions! They are runaway thoughts that will lead you down roads you should not go down.

But the questions are not bad. They force you to address real issues, and that is actually good for you. Why? Because:

> Until we have dealt with and can manage our doubts, we cannot be totally committed to our business.

Hit those questions and thoughts head on! Don't back down. Face to face, address the issues, because in so doing you are strengthening your resolve to win! That is, of course, a very good thing and it will serve you well for years to come.

How to Fight Smart

You want to address issues in such a way that you (metaphorically speaking) put them under your feet so that you can stand on them to reach higher and go further. That is the goal.

But in reality, some days are just bad days. That is a fact of life. It is also dangerous, for:

> *When you bring fear and worry into your life, you start to decrease your ability to think clearly and rationally, and therefore you are less productive.*

If only you could put those days on "pause" and address the issue another time … but you can! I call these bad days "hold days."

On "hold days," you do not make any major decisions because you are too emotional and you are not thinking clearly. Remind yourself that tomorrow will be a better day. That is fighting smart.

When everything is going right, just as you planned, I call these days "banner days." On "banner days," you are not as emotional, you should be able to make rational decisions, and because you have less worry and stress, you are also much more productive. Those are great, confidence-building days!

It's tempting to make your big decisions on these peak-like "banner days," but I recommend that you not make any major decisions on "banner days," just as you don't on "hold days," until you are experiencing at least 80% of your days as "banner days."

To summarize ... make your decisions when your normal day is a good day and you are emotionally steady, you are rational, and you are not worried or stressed out. That is fighting smart!

Change the Blame Game

If we fail in the financial world, we tend to blame the market, Wall Street, our financial advisor, and even that co-worker who helped us choose the investments for our company's 401K.

For some reason, it has been drilled into our heads that it is best if we never take responsibility for our actions or decisions, especially if the choices we made were disappointing.

Well, that is no longer an option! Here is your new reality:

> *If you are going to be in business, you must take on the responsibility of your actions and your decisions.*

This means a change of mindset, and when you think this way, you become someone who is both confident and competent. And as a result, you **will** become successful and those around you **will** notice!

> *Success is the difference between a winner and a whiner!*

When I was young and starting out in business, a wise man told me that when you fail it is because you have **chosen** to fail. I wasn't sure I agreed with him until he explained how we usually try to rationalize a way to quit. Saying, "I quit," is to choose to fail.

I was still thinking about those words when he asked me, "Do you want to see where the problem lies, every single time?"

"Sure," I replied.

He answered, "Then look in the mirror."

I was about to say something else when he added, "Want to see where the answer is to those same problems, each and every time?"

"For sure," I exclaimed.

"Then look in the mirror," he stated with a smile.

Years later, I have found what he said to be 100% accurate. It's the truth. So change the blame game once and for all. Choose to take responsibility and be the winner that you know you are!

You Have What It Takes

You are the businessperson who did the homework, you analyzed your business idea thoroughly, you engaged professionals to help you decide what insurances you needed, you set up a business entity that made sense, and you are the one who did the hard work.

All that is because:

> You are the person who believes in you the most!

What's more, you are the one who has what it takes to adapt to new and different ideas and situations. What works today may or may not work tomorrow, and you are the one who will see it and probably be the first person to see it.

And when you make mistakes, because you will no doubt make mistakes, learn quickly so you never repeat them.

Michael Jordan insightfully used to say, "A loss is not failure until you make an excuse." I like that, and it fits well with what it takes to be successful in business.

No more excuses. Take responsibility. And work smarter. Why will that work?

> You have what it takes because you are the one most committed to making your company successful.

Look to Improve

Always keep an eye out for possible improvements. Many of your ideas at first seem like they are the best and the only way to do something, but given enough time and experience, you will definitely see that some of those ideas or methods were not necessarily the best.

Be open to that type of improvement. It shows you are smart and humble at the same time!

I see it like picking up sea shells at the beach. At first, most any sea shell is good enough and it goes in the basket, but after a while, you start to get more and more selective about the shells you pick up. Only the best unbroken shells will be good enough. You may even choose certain colors and sizes, even further refining the selection process, which means you will probably throw out most of what you previously collected.

In business, experience is the best teacher, so you are becoming better by looking for ways to improve. However, this refining process can be good or bad.

If your new set of standards means you make a product or service better for your customers or clients, then I applaud your efforts. Good job, and keep it up.

On the other hand, if these new standards tend to make you forget why you were passionate enough to start your business in the first place and your products or services are not keeping in line with what is best for your customers or clients, then you need to get back to your plan.

This is not to say that your plan cannot be changed or modified as your experience and knowledge develops. Of course not … but if you are going to change your focus or standards significantly, then rework your plan and write new standards to your business plan, and then discuss these changes with your legal and accounting professionals.

Looking to improve in all you do means you are improving the lives of your customers or clients. Always keep that in mind.

A little test:

> *Do you do things for others, like your clients, and not look for something in return?*

If you are still doing that for your clients, then you are still on the right path.

You Reap What You Sow

When I was young, my mother would say, "You need to make sure you work hard, because you reap what you sow."

No doubt you heard this or a similar phrase from someone in your past, maybe even *your* mother, but no matter how it was said, all parents try to teach their children the value of a good work ethic.

I've practiced sowing and reaping for decades and here is how I see it:

- You reap the same thing you sow. If you sow wheat, you reap wheat.
- You always reap more than you sow. A few kernels of corn will result in multiple ears with hundreds of kernels.
- You never reap in the same season as you sow. Your efforts today will reap rewards in the future, such as business relationships, personal relationships, advancement, education, etc.

It is true:

You will reap what you sow, so you might as well sow the best possible seeds you can!

CHAPTER FIVE

CREATING VALUE

In the business world, "creating value" is a phrase that is thrown around a lot, but what exactly is value? By definition, value is the present worth of anticipated future benefits.

There are many different types of value, such as replacement value, liquidating value, market value, appraised value, insurance value, assessed value, location value, salvage value, intrinsic value, exchange value, and investment value. Then something could have value to a single person, value to groups of people, value to a business, value to a country, and so on.

Basically, you can identify something, come up with reasons why it has value, and you have suddenly created value. Yes, that means the opportunity to create value is endless!

To prove my point, choose something small, seemingly insignificant. Have you thought of something? If not, I will, and I choose the lowly rock.

Now, you list reasons why your thing is valuable or has value. I can think of countless reasons why rocks are valuable.

Almost immediately, you can no doubt see that creating value in virtually anything is very easy. My rocks, for example, are necessary for road construction, do-it-yourself (DIY) projects at home, soil erosion, grinding into pebbles or sand, and much more.

The more difficult task is to come up with enough reasons on your list that are also of true value to other people. You think it's of value, but will they? The more reasons you have or the bigger the reasons you have, the greater potential your business has for success.

The Value You Want to Create

When you look at value in business, there are two categories that everything basically falls into. That is:

#1 — Value in Use

#2 — Value in Exchange

At its core, value in use is a subjective value. It's harder to quantify the exact value, thus making it subjective. Salvage value and insurance value are examples of this.

Value in exchange, on the other hand, is objective. It is more of an exact value something has to others. Market value, appraised value, and business value are good examples.

Which value are you going to create to make your business successful? Is it value in **use** or value in **exchange**?

Prosperity is achieved by creating value, which means:

> *When you build your business, make sure that the value you are creating is the value in exchange.*

To generate the business you want, it requires that you create *value in exchange*. You accomplish that through the principals of D.U.S.T.

> **D: demand** – Is there a demand for the products or services you are providing now, and will that need continue into the future?

> **U: understanding** – Will an investor see the value in your company or is your idea(s) too hard to manage or explain?

> **S: stability** – Is your company stable, or is your company underfunded? Furthermore, is your company building equity?

T: *transferability* – Does the company you have built have a "brand identity" so that when an investor looks at your company, it will stand out among the best in your area or expertise? Can your company be transferred to others easily, and are there any tax advantages with this transfer?

When you apply D.U.S.T. to your business, you are creating value that translates into financial gain. That is because you have all the necessary elements for success!

Selling Your Business

If you decide to sell your business in the distant future, keep in mind that no one (in their right mind) is going to pay more for your company than they can go to the market and purchase.

Sometimes you will hear of someone paying more for a business than it is seems worth, but if you dig further, you will find that some *value in use* was added into the purchase price.

Now, don't read me wrong, value in use is not a bad thing. But if you build your business on the foundation of *value in exchange*, when you do sell your company, the perceived *value in use* is a bonus! Remember this principle:

If you honestly create value, you will attain true wealth.

Consider some big-name companies like Microsoft, IBM, Apple, Ford, Walmart, Geico, Chic-fil-A, McDonalds, Mars, Pepsi, and countless others. Think about how the products those companies produce make our lives better or more enjoyable.

But no matter how "huge" the companies seem today, what types of struggles do you think the founders lived through? No doubt they faced obstacles when they began, unsure of themselves and how their products or services would be received. If you have those same feelings, then you are in good company!

Price Does NOT Equal Value

It is important to understand that price is not value. New or inexperienced entrepreneurs often get confused when discussing this comparison. They have been so conditioned to focus on price that they forget to consider value.

Now, price is obviously important, but it is only part of a larger pie. When making important financial decisions, you must consider all parts or features of your business, not only a small piece. Failure to do so is to be paralyzed in your thinking, and that stifles your creativity.

For example, think about a football team. Before the ball is even snapped out on the field, the coaches have run scenarios on the passing game, running game, getting to a first down position, getting close enough to score, the weakest players, etc. If all or most of these parts are working together, the team wins. If not, they don't. It's simple math!

Using the wisdom of the coaches and self-discipline of the players brings order to the entire effort. This consistent "order" builds trust within the team and dependability among players, and the players begin to make conscious choices to do their best. It is a contagious winning attitude that only gets better and better … but it's on all the pieces working together.

You are that team, and the more you can get all your pieces working together in sync, the greater your chances for success.

That is value, and it is worth its weight in gold!

CHAPTER SIX

YOUR FINANCIAL SECURITY

Say the words "financial security" and everyone has a different definition these days. My grandparents used to think CDs were the way to go, but my parents used to tell me, "Buy land because they are not making any more dirt." Others swear that gold is the way to go.

Bring up the subject to financial advisors and they will say, "Whatever you do, diversify," all while recommending mutual funds, annuities, bonds, options, and other financial instruments that help diversify your portfolio.

Interestingly, nobody recommends a small business as a means of financial security.

Small Business for Financial Security

Why don't financial advisors tell their clients to invest in small businesses? The biggest reason is that financial advisors don't understand the small business world.

Being a small business owner is a rare breed. What type of person is going to invest in themselves so heavily that they will "bet the farm" on their own success? They will get up in the morning before everyone else and go to bed usually after everyone else does.

Sounds fun, right? But financial advisors don't get it, and that is fine. Don't expect them to understand what you do or what fuels your motivation. But I repeat … if done right, your small business will probably be the most rewarding adventure you will ever take!

Is There Financial Security?

You may have heard or been told that by simply being in business and working for yourself you will somehow achieve financial security. Those who say that, with no experiential knowledge, have no clue.

At the other end of the spectrum, I have heard people say that working for a large company or a government agency will give you the most financial security.

I disagree. In my opinion:

> *There is no true financial security. None whatsoever!*

With the devaluation of the dollar, market fluctuations, social security on the brink of disaster, states going broke, businesses closing, and more, how can we put our trust in anyone or anything?

Even the hesitation to invest your hard-earned funds is to take on additional risks!

What are we to do? There are several things we can do:

- Remember when we discussed earlier that when you fail you choose to fail because you said, "I quit?" Failure is a choice, so choose to be totally committed.
- Diversifying is a must. Never put all your eggs in one basket.
- Maintain a positive attitude. Take a moment and look in the face of a loved one. Maybe it's a child or a grandchild. Listen to the hope in their voice and see the sparkle in their eyes for a better and brighter tomorrow. When I do this, I truly believe the world is in good hands.
- Stay healthy so you can function like you need to and care for others.
- Have trust and faith in yourself, in others, and in this country. You need to remember to keep these ideals at the forefront of all your decisions.

Combined, these are the closest thing to financial security that I know of.

Pursue your dreams with all the passion you have. This is your one chance to chase your dreams. Don't let the words of others or the situations around you dissuade you in any way.

As you know, the best form of financial security is yourself!

CHAPTER SEVEN

UPDATING YOUR BUSINESS OPERATIONS

At this point, maybe your business is already humming along or maybe you are still putting the pieces together. Either way, here is a truth that will be of value to you right here and now:

Make sure you continue to update your business plan.

Keep It All Updated

The "continue to update your business plan" is a detail that is often forgotten. Why? Here are two big reasons why not:

#1 – I don't need to: The business owners feel they have made it far enough down the road and their business is doing well that updating the business plan is no longer important. They don't think they need to.

CHAPTER EIGHT

LIVING YOUR BUSINESS ETHICS

What does it mean to truly have an ethical business and to operate with ethical behavior? That is really a good question that each of us must answer.

The answers vary as everyone seems to have their own definition. To some, being ethical means:

- Treating people fairly
- Paying your taxes
- Not acting selfishly
- Never misrepresenting your product or service
- Recommending products that truly benefit people
- Doing what is right, even when no one is looking
- Being the kind of person your dog thinks you are

If you discuss ethical behavior, key moral principles such as honesty, fairness, equality, dignity, diversity, and individual rights will inevitably come up.

It's all important because the fact is:

Ethical behavior is good for business!

The opposite is just as true. A business that folds due to unethical behavior is not only sad, it is a completely unnecessary occurrence in my books! If only the owners had been ethical, they would probably be in business today.

It makes sense (and cents) to be ethical, but you would be surprised at how some people act, all while working so hard to grow their dream business. So do yourself a huge favor and be ethical. It really pays to do just that.

I personally define ethical behavior as this:

Always doing what is right, not necessarily what is popular.

However you define ethical behavior, the point is that when you build your business, always be honest and consistent when handling your affairs. You cannot go wrong with that!

Here is the fastest way to see if you are acting in an ethical way:

Ask yourself, "Would I do business with me?"

If your answer is an immediate "absolutely," then you are on your way. Good job, and keep at it.

If there is a hesitancy, an excuse, or some other form of hedging, then you are in trouble and probably won't be in business for long. Unethical businesses cannot flourish.

Being ethical is not a *sometimes* thing ... it is an *everyday* thing.

Industry-Specific Ethics

Most professions have their own set of ethical standards that dictate what is acceptable behavior for their professionals. This could be measurements, weights, accounting methods, schedules, ingredients, sizes, disclosures, or some other detail that is deemed important.

Whatever the industry states, do that ... and a little bit more! You want the reputation of being a business leader who *always* does what is right.

That type of reputation is worth its weight in gold, many times over!

CHAPTER NINE

CREATING A LEGACY

You may be wondering why I would talk about legacy in the middle of a business book. "Shouldn't it be discussed at the end?" you ask.

I'm a believer that we should always begin with the end in mind. Also, I have found that:

You hit what you aim at.

With that said, now is always the perfect time to talk about the legacy you are leaving behind.

What Type of Legacy Are You Leaving?

We are all leaving a legacy. The question is what type of legacy are we leaving?

A legacy, according to the dictionary, is simply something that is handed down from the past, most likely from an ancestor. That definition fails to give us any insight on how to go about *creating* a legacy.

When I talk about creating a business legacy, I am talking about two things:

#1 – Worth Money: Creating a business that can be passed down to those who come after you. They can either run it or sell it.

#2 – Worth Copying: Making a business that others want to copy. How you built it and what you built, all of it is a good model worth replicating.

Your legacy will grow and change with each new experience, but keep these two principles in mind. They will serve you well.

Your Legacy Through Others

One powerful aspect of a legacy is the fact that a legacy lives through others. You invest in people, and they help build and live out your legacy.

This is why mentoring is so powerful. Yes, you are impacting another person's life and bettering them in some way. You may be imparting business concepts, explanations, solutions, reasons, and features that help that person and business grow, but you (the mentor) are the one who benefits the most.

I can tell you from personal experience that this is true. Years ago, when I owned a real estate appraisal firm, I was always looking for additional revenue sources. I learned I could get certified and teach appraisal classes, so I did that, but in doing so I discovered that the many local schools graduated you but never actually gave you any practical experience in appraising a property.

It only made sense that the students with no guidance or direction would not last long in the industry. I immediately started teaching appraisal classes that included a licensed appraiser taking the students into the field and showing them how to appraise a property.

As a result, these better-trained appraisers were immediate hires for my company, and business took off. Talk about exponential growth! And it came as I invested in others. They benefited, but I benefited even more.

A friend of mine showed me a poem that really captures the essence of leaving a legacy behind:

> If you want to be Happy for an Hour
> *– take a nap*
> If you want to be Happy for a Day
> *– go golfing*
> If you want to be Happy for a Week
> *– take a trip*
> If you want to be Happy for a Year
> *– inherit money*
> If you want to be Happy for a Lifetime
> *– be an asset to others*

I don't know about you, but I want to be happy for a lifetime.

Keep on Building Your Legacy

Distractions abound when it comes to building your legacy. You will find them in the form of other people asking (or you wondering) such things as:

- Can I keep this up?
- Is it time to quit?
- Should I get out while the getting is good?

Don't let it get to you, and remember to think like a businessperson! Consider all aspects of your decision. When I was in my mid-40s, my business was doing great and I wondered to myself, "Maybe it's time for me to sell out and retire."

That sounded pretty good for a few minutes ... and then reality set in. I had three teenagers to educate, pay for weddings, and whatever else that would inevitably come along, not to mention eventual grandkids many years down the road.

Needless to say, after breaking out in a cold sweat, I quickly came back to reality! I threw out the thoughts of selling and doubled down, looking for ways to make what I did more profitable. In hindsight, it worked out well that I didn't try to sell. My business grew and my assets grew 100 fold.

Remember:

> When you are considering making a life-changing business or retirement decision, always think like a businessperson.

Your legacy will take shape as you work hard (the necessary blood, sweat, and tears part) and overcome disappointments along your road to a successful business.

Yes, "success" is spelled W-O-R-K. Some say a 40-hour week is hard work, but you no doubt know (or you will soon find out) that 60 or 80 hours a week is probably more accurate.

I have found that:

> You have to do today what other people are not willing to do ... so you can have tomorrow what others will not be able to have.

It takes consistent effort over time to build a lasting legacy, so keep at it.

Is There an End?

There is a time and a place to sell, step down, retire, or move on. These questions may help you in making the tough decisions:

#1 – Is it still fun and/or rewarding? The answer should certainly be a resounding "yes." That does not mean you have to work the long hours or take on as much risk, but it should still be fun and rewarding for you. If it's not fun, then your business is still a work in progress.

#2 – Are you still passionate about it? The answer should also be "yes" because you are doing what you enjoy. If not, why not?

#3 – Do you have peace of mind? Are you making a difference in life? Are you positively impacting the lives of those around you? Again, I would expect a "yes" from you on this one.

If you can answer "yes" to all of these questions, then you should feel good about the legacy you have achieved or are building. Mind you, that doesn't mean you need to sell it! Treat that thought with your best business mind possible.

A resounding "yes" to all three questions simply means you have built something worthwhile. For that, congratulations are in store.

Well done!

CHAPTER TEN

GENERATING REFERRALS

With sufficient numbers of the "right" referrals, your business success is almost guaranteed! That is the power of referrals, and that is also why it is such an important part of your business.

The art of building a client or customer base is admittedly pretty diverse. There are a lot of methods to use, depending on what type of business or industry you are in.

For example, if you are in a wholesale, retail, or mail order business, you are looking for entirely different clients, so your approach to getting those clients will also be different. Or maybe your business is a professional or fee-for-service business. That also means a different type of client or customer base and thus a unique approach.

Some professions have restrictions on how and what type of advertising and soliciting techniques can be used to obtain potential clients.

Regardless of the unique business or specific customers you may need, there is one truth for all businesses — past, present, and future:

You need a steady influx of new business.

Without referrals, a business is doomed ... but with a lot of new referrals, the sky is the limit! Literally, unlimited success is tied up in the art of getting referrals.

What to do?

Which method to choose?

The choice is yours, and it's a choice you must make, but I will tell you the one method of referral getting that I know will work in every type of businesses. It doesn't matter if your business is retail, wholesale, professional, fee-based, or with little or no restrictions. That proven referral method is this:

Always ask for referrals.

In my experience, this is the absolute best and yet most overlooked method of getting referrals. It is also the easiest and cheapest of all the methods!

It's amazing, the more often you ask for referrals, the easier it gets! Since I have made it a practice to ask for referrals each and every time I meet with clients, many times my regular clients bring in a list of a few names to refer! Though they may love me, I think the real reason they come with their referral list is because they know I'm going to ask for referrals and they want to be prepared, and that makes them feel good.

Either way, it's great. You want those referrals!

The Heart of Your Company

Remember when I said that your working capital was the "life-blood" of your company? Well, referrals are the "heart" of your company. If you can create a method of getting referrals that flows with your working capital, creating a positive cash flow at the other end, then you are on your way!

If you haven't already done so, you need to clarify your referral-getting method. Write it out, tweak it, and put it to work. This is something that will probably need to be updated more frequently than annually. Things change, new opportunities arise, so always keep looking for new ways to bring in more referrals.

Always Think for Yourself

Getting referrals is to have a mindset that is always saying, "How can I get more business?"

While you do that, keep in mind that you must always think for yourself. Sounds pretty logical, but there are times when it is very tempting to let someone else do the thinking for you. Resist that urge!

Here is why:

Getting burned hurts!

Years ago, as my businesses grew and my management teams became more experienced, I kept my eye out for ways to diversify my company. Specifically, I would look for businesses I could buy to increase our diversity and cash flow.

I knew that thinking for myself and drawing on the experience of some of our trusted employees was a smart move. I also knew that doing our due diligence, pro formas, etc. was still a necessary part of the process. Sadly, once I failed to keep my own requirements!

In one meeting with my management team, the head of accounting said there was a small ice cream shop in the local community that was for sale. The investment was only $25,000.

"But I know nothing about the ice cream business," I objected.

He smiled and said, "Not to worry, boss, I have that covered. I used to be with a large dairy company as the sales manager. There is a ton of money to be made in the ice cream business!"

Well, I thought I had hit the jackpot! I told him to put the deal together and we would look at it.

My first mistake was not thinking for myself. I should have thought it through and not given my chief accountant the job of thinking for me. His advice, it turned out, was far less valuable than I expected.

My second mistake was that I did not fully understand what a "sales manager" for a dairy company really was. I found out that he was a route salesman. While I don't have a problem with route salesmen, I thought I was getting advice from someone who had experience managing sales ... and not someone who stocked the shelves at four grocery stores.

My third mistake was the time and money lost in the deal, but I won't go there. This was my mistake. I can't blame anyone else for my own stupidity. But my advice to you:

> *If you don't think for yourself, you will fall into the same trap.*

Thinking for yourself does not give you 100% foolproof protection, but it is certainly a good safeguard from common scams, pitfalls, and money drains. Believe me when I say that thinking for yourself is an absolute must!

Thankfully, we can all learn from our mistakes.

I sure did!

CHAPTER ELEVEN

TAKING YOUR BUSINESS TO THE NEXT LEVEL

You may be well past the setting up stage and well into running a successful business. If so, you are probably more than ready to raise the bar and take your business to the next level.

Climbing Even Higher

What does it take to get to the next level? It is going to require an increase in your sales, an increase in your client/customer base, and an increase in your profits.

I will tell you, going to the next level has its prerequisites:

> *Taking your business to the next level can only be done if you are determined, have a good reputation, and build strong relationships with your clients or customers.*

Those who fail to meet the prerequisites will also fail to reach the next level. That's just the way it is.

The pro forma documents you originally created to give your "best guess" or "what if" scenario of your future growth was necessary when you started. Now, however, it is time to think about and address your new needs ... that of taking things to the next level!

Next Level Steps

You are a more "seasoned" business owner now, and that means you need to take some additional steps that will help take your business even higher.

Let's begin with an exercise. I want you to write down (briefly stated is fine) the top five business concerns/goals you would like to overcome/accomplish:

- _____
- _____
- _____
- _____
- _____

After you have made your list (above), it is time to rank them (below) in the order of their importance.

1. _____
2. _____

3. _____

4. _____

5. _____

The law of next-level growth that you need to keep in mind is this:

> *If you always do what you've always done, you'll get what you've always gotten.*

Maybe you need a new or different way of managing or marketing your business or service. Or maybe it is time to practice your presentation skills. Whatever it is that you know you need to work on, you should also take some time to visit with other colleagues or staff to make sure your ideas and approaches aren't outdated.

Has your business kept up with new technology? Have you maintained your business ethics? Have you practiced good customer service? Have you worked to keep the communication lines open? If we will pay attention, almost everyone has something they can teach us.

All the little details we have discussed along the way, each of them plays a part in the overall success of your business … and in the preparation to take things to the next level.

Regarding the "little details," I have found:

The little things are either a foundation to your success or stumbling blocks that will trip you up.

Master the little things so you can move on and take things to the next level.

The VIDA Method

With every business I started, bought, or was a part of, I applied the VIDA method to it.

With this method, you will manage your business or company by combining your values, ideas, determination, and attitudes. It is a powerful and yet practical combination that always benefits everyone involved.

It looks like this:

V: Values

- Do I understand integrity?
- Do I have the client's best interest in mind?
- Do I do what I say I'm going to do?

I: Ideas

- Are you willing to accept new ideas?
- Or is your mind closed to things you think you can't learn?
- Or do you refuse to learn?

D: Determination

- Are you determined to do better?
- Are you willing to learn new ways that will enhance your own style?

A: Attitudes

- Do you have a positive attitude toward your job?
- Toward the clients or customers you see?
- Toward the company you represent?
- Or do you need an attitude adjustment?

In my opinion, by following this method you will not fail!

Final Push

After you have applied the VIDA method to your business and worked through the 5 concerns/goals, and if you are still not seeing the improvement you want and need, then sit down with other colleagues in the business, your CPA, and your attorney.

These individuals have been on your team from the beginning, and of all people they can give you valuable insights into what needs to be done to take your business to the next level. Their advice is invaluable.

Getting to the next level is not usually an instant or easy process. Stick to it ... you'll get there, I'm confident of that!

CHAPTER TWELVE

Handling Risks

Taking risks is something that most people prefer to avoid. Some say they are "adverse" to it, while others admit they are flat-out scared of taking risks. In truth, there are risks everywhere, in every profession, and being right or wrong is even a risk.

Most advisors will tell you that when you increase your chances of winning, you are also increasing your chances of losing. Is it a risk worth taking?

You Can't Avoid Risk

The longer you have been in business, the more you know that business is full of risks … on a daily basis!

I have found:

> *If you know nothing about a product, service, or investment, then it is risky.*

Thankfully the opposite also holds true:

If you know a lot about a product, service, or investment, then it may not be as risky for you.

As we discussed already, there are certain inherent risks you must investigate and understand as you set up your business. Also, since you have met the team you have assembled to address things like insurance, accounting, legal issues, etc., the "normal" business risks of simply being in business have been addressed.

Basically, you can mitigate most risks by making sure you are well-informed about the subject. In other words:

The more you know, the less the risk.

Transfer the Risk

Being in business does not in any way mean that you recklessly take on more risk than you should. That is not only unwise, it is foolish! It is also unnecessary.

Successful businesspeople practice risk management by doing something that few people have even considered. Their secret? They transfer the risk!

I have had successful businesspeople tell me that they would have never been able to accumulate the wealth they have today ... if they hadn't learned the art of transferring risk to a third party.

They explain:

Retaining risks that could have been transferred severely reduces your ability to produce at the level you are really going to want to and possibly need to perform at.

Transfer unnecessary risk ... sounds smart, considering the source! This means doing everything in your power to limit as many of the normal business uncertainties as possible. It only makes sense:

> If you can eliminate or at least reduce your risk, do it.

These are insurable risks, and you need to think long and hard about such risks. If you can transfer the risk to a third party, I suggest that you do it.

Risks That Should NOT Be Risks

There are some risks that really should not be risks in the first place. These are what I call "no brainer" risks that you can deal with and move past, never giving them a chance to pose a risk for you.

These risks are not insurable risks. They cannot be transferred. These are the risks that can be avoided if you will:

- Stop
- Think
- Evaluate
- Decide

Sounds simple enough, but you would be surprised at how many businesses go under or fail to perform up to their potential, all because they got caught up in these unnecessary risks. The good news is that it does not need to happen to you!

A perfect example of one of these unnecessary risks would be spending down your bank account without considering that you have to pay your payroll in two days. As you recall, this should be a non-issue because as a good businessperson you preserved your working capital.

Another example is purchasing too much inventory without considering the time of year it is or where to store it. As you remember, having the shelves full of products that can expire is not wise, but you have already taken steps to not do that.

Yet another example is treating customers poorly, such as overcharging them for services they do not need. Not only does this mean the loss of a customer, and a potential legal battle, but it also destroys all chances of getting referrals. This goes against business sense, as well as your agreed-upon ethical principles ... but again, you would be surprised how many companies do this!

There are countless other examples of no-brainer risks that are not really risks at all. Stick to the principles you started with and these types of risks will not even be a concern.

Decision-Making

Decision-making is obviously something that you have to do, every day, all day, with no breaks. It can be tiring, but the more you do it, the better you will get at it.

My father gave me some great decision-making advice that has served me well for many years. He said:

> Each time you make a decision, ask yourself, "What's the worst that can happen?" And if you are okay with that, then do it.

For example, let's say I pull up to a convenience store and leave the car running while I run in to get a soda. When I come back, my car is gone.

I don't like that scenario, so I turn the car off and go inside. When I come back, someone is in the back seat.

I don't like that scenario either! So considering the worst that could happen, I turn the car off, lock the doors, and go in … and when I come back, the car should be the same as I left it.

We all think like this as we go about our daily tasks, analyze facts, and make decisions. It comes naturally, and rightly it should.

I have found:

> *The better you are in managing your risks, the happier you will be.*

If you get stuck in business, reapply your business principles that have helped guide you. Then ask yourself, "What is the worst that can happen?" If you are good with it, then go for it!

CHAPTER THIRTEEN

KNOWING YOUR DEBTS AND LIABILITIES

We have talked a lot about business and implementing those ideas and procedures to make your business as successful as it can be. What we have not talked about is the distinction between debt and liabilities.

Most people think they are one in the same, and though they do have a few similar characteristics, there are other features that are completely different.

It is these "other features" that can get you in trouble.

Understanding Debt

We have all been taught that debt is:

- A duty or obligation
- To deliver goods, render services, or pay money
- As your agreement states

That is it. Pretty basic. And if you owe, you are the debtor/debitor. If the goods, services, or money are owed to you, then you are the debtee/creditor/lender.

Using debt to create financial leverage that results in profits is how businesses use debt to their advantage. And since interest paid on debt can be written off as an expense, using debt to grow a business is one of the most economical and long-term methods to do just that.

Understanding Liability

Liability, on the other hand, is defined as:

- An obligation
- That legally binds you to settle a debt

If you are liable for a debt, that means you are the one responsible for paying that debt. Or if some wrongful act occurred, and you are liable, that means you are responsible for it.

Legally, if you are liable, you are bound to it. You will have to pay up.

Where Debt and Liability Impact You

Debt and liability affect your business every single day in many different ways. I won't repeat the obvious. Rather, I want to bring your attention to two different areas where your debt and liability have a way of impacting you.

#1 Impact – Your Wealth: When we talk about wealth, we are talking about all the assets that you or the company have. You add up the market value for the physical and intangible assets (a building, piece of property, inventory, database, etc.) and then subtract out all the debt.

It is the debt that can really undermine the perceived wealth that you or the company supposedly have. Be careful with that, and make sure you do the math.

Furthermore, remember when we talked about the different types of business entities? Make sure you understand the type of liability you have assumed with the business entity you have chosen.

#2 Impact – Making a Profit: Years ago, I hired a guy who was referred to me to help in pricing and managing expenses. He seemed like a sharp guy. Early on in his employment, he came to me and said we should stock a particular product because we could sell the product at a good price.

I had already explained our sales margins and cost of goods sold, so I didn't feel the need to repeat myself … and you can probably imagine what happened!

Well, the products did fly off the shelves! Everyone was so excited. And then I got the invoice from the vendor. I couldn't believe what I was reading! We were selling the product for a mere 3% markup!

I thought I would have a heart attack! I brought him in and tried to understand what was going on. I reiterated how margins worked and how important it was to make sure we priced products so we can pay our bills and stay in business.

He stammered, "I figured any amount over the cost of the product was a profit."

Again, I had no one to blame but myself, for I let him do my thinking. I don't think (even after I explained it for the 12th time) that he ever understood that profits were not profits until all expenses were deducted out.

Don't ever let this reality slip from the front of your mind:

> *A real profit is what is left over after all costs associated with all business operations have been deducted.*

If nothing is left over, then there are no profits! That was the case with my 3% markup guy. Needless to say, his employment with my firm was short-lived.

So whether you are talking debt or liability, both affect you and your business in countless ways. Don't ever forget that.

CHAPTER FOURTEEN

YOUR DEFINING MOMENTS

Life is full of choices. Everything, really, is a choice, which means each of us has a unique opportunity each and every day to make the right choices.

It is not about being perfect, but about doing better, making better choices, repeatedly.

The results can be truly amazing.

The Small Things

In business, as well as in life, I have found this to be true:

You usually get out of it what you put into it.

Years ago, my father was at the office helping me work on some details for an expansion move. I was talking with a supervisor in my office discussing the day's agenda when my father knocked on the door.

When he opened the door, I responded by saying, "Yes, what's the problem?"

He paused for a second, then walked in and asked if he could speak with me in private. The supervisor slipped out quickly.

My father came around my desk where I was standing and got right up in my face and said sternly, "Does everything with you have to be a da** problem? Maybe there was an opportunity I wanted to talk with you about, but you turned it into a problem."

I was shaken up a bit. I wondered to myself, "Am I really that negative?" I was, after all, the company's problem solver. We were all busy, so whenever my door opened, I would get right to the point and ask, "What's the problem?"

Up until that moment, I had never given much thought about how it sounded or how others perceived my statement. I wasn't trying to be negative, but it sounded that way!

After a few days, I came to the conclusion that I needed to change. My goal was to build the company as big as possible, and that meant I needed to be sure that everyone was on the same page and that everyone felt good about each other.

I knew:

As the leader, they will follow your lead.

Right then and there, I chose to change how I responded to others. It was a little thing, what I said when the door opened, but it would make a bigger impact than I expected.

Honestly, it was hard to believe how that positive attitude spread throughout the entire company. My little attitude adjustment helped transform my company!

Your Defining Moments

We all have these defining moments. They happen usually when we least expect them, but the positive change that comes as a result cannot be refuted.

It's like a brick to the head that brings about change. My suggestion:

> *If you get hit on the head, make sure it doesn't happen again. Change now!*

If you have forgotten the past few defining moments in your business life, it is good for you to be reminded. Take a second to jot down the past three defining moments you have experienced:

1. _____
2. _____
3. _____

Every successful entrepreneur has those defining moments and uses them to help take things to the next level.

CHAPTER FIFTEEN

HIRING CORRECTLY

Attracting good quality employees is always a challenge. My father used to say, "If you want good help, you have to steal them from another company." I don't know if I 100% agree, but it is indeed tough to find and then keep good employees.

Such is the challenge of every business owner.

I asked an extremely successful businessman one time how he prevented employee turnover. He said:

> I used to have a lot of turnover until I started treating employees as assets. Once I did, both my attitude and the employees' attitudes changed. It was amazing! Everyone was more positive, and it became an even better place to work.

Good advice! What's more, that is a way to maximize your employees' potential, and when you empower them to be prosperous, they will win ... and so will you!

Know the Rules of Questioning

When it comes to hiring, there is a process and set rules of hiring that you must keep in mind. If you don't, you will get in trouble!

I have to confess that I stink at this!

When I used to hire employees, I would ask all sorts of questions (are you married, do you have any children, do you smoke, do you have any problem working late, etc.) that would get me sued today.

Again, hiring is not supposed to be a risk for you and your business. Keep that in mind. Quite simply:

> *Familiarize yourself with what questions are legally acceptable to ask so you keep yourself away from potential lawsuits.*

Back in the late 70s, I was trying to hire a few delivery drivers for our company. We had just purchased several new trucks and I was bound and determined to try and keep the trucks looking like new as long as possible. The old trucks had cigarette holes in the seats, coffee and sodas spilled on the seats and dashes, and knobs were missing on the consul electronics.

When I placed an ad in the newspaper, I said only non-smokers needed apply. One guy showed up for the interview with a pack of cigarettes in his shirt pocket.

I said to him, "You are a non-smoker, right?"

He replied, "Absolutely."

When I pointed at the pack of cigarettes and said, "Isn't that a pack of cigarettes?"

He put his hand over his pocket and said, "Yes it is, but if this job requires me to be a non-smoker, then I guess I'm a non-smoker."

Needless to say, he was not hired.

I know those types of questions would no longer be allowed, so thank goodness I'm not interviewing candidates any longer. I don't know if I could handle it!

The Taboo of Specific Questions

Below are interview questions (and to prove I did not make this up, it comes from Minnesota Department of Employment and Economic Development) that you can and cannot ask. Make sure you follow these guidelines:

Legal Interview Questions:

- What education do you have?
- What experience qualifies you for this job?
- Do you have licenses and certifications for this job?
- Are you willing to travel?
- What name(s) are your work records under?
- Do you have the legal right to work in the United States?
- Are you available for overtime?

Legal Requests for Information After Hiring Questions:

- A copy of your birth certificate
- Affirmative action statistics
- Your marital status (married or single only)
- Proof of citizenship
- Photographs
- Physical examination and drug testing
- Social Security card

Illegal Interview Questions:

Some questions are illegal for an employer to ask before a conditional offer of employment. These may include the following questions:

- What is your age or date of birth?
- What is your sexual orientation?

- What church do you attend?
- What is your national origin?
- What is your maiden name?
- What is your marital status?
- Are you widowed, divorced, or separated?
- What is or was your spouse's name and/or job?
- Have you ever filed a workers' compensation claim?
- Do you have any physical impairments or disabilities that would prevent you from performing the job for which you are applying?

Title I of the American Disabilities Act (ADA) lists these additional *prohibited* questions:

- Have you ever been hospitalized? If so, for what condition?
- Have you ever been treated by a psychiatrist or psychologist? If so, for what condition?
- Is there any health-related reason that you may not be able to perform the job for which you are applying?
- How many days were you absent from work because of illness last year?
- Are you taking any prescribed drugs?
- Have you ever been treated for drug addiction or alcoholism?

Bottom line, make sure you and your interview people understand what questions they can and cannot ask in an interview.

Clarify Expectations

Make sure you communicate clearly about what you want employees to do. Back in the 80s, I was hiring an accounting person for my company. I explained how we were a small company and that everyone pitched in and I asked an interviewee if he was willing to help out in the shipping department after hours if it got backed up. He said he was.

Well, I hired the guy and that first day on the job the shipping department got behind. Everyone in the office stayed after 5:00 p.m. to help load. But the new guy never showed.

The next day, I asked the new accountant if he had a problem working late. In the interview, he said he had no problem with it.

He replied, "No, I don't have a problem working late, I just can't because I have law school at 5:30 p.m. every night."

I learned a valuable lesson that day!

Be very clear in your communications with employees and candidates. A good idea is to put together an employee contract and handbook. By spelling out job descriptions and company philosophy, you can avoid potential misunderstandings.

It is a good idea to:

Put all questions and concerns on the table.

When in doubt, spell it out.

Watch Your Words!

I knew I was never the best person in the company to do the interviews, but I did them for years anyway. I didn't want to give my thinking away to others. As time went along, I was only involved in a small portion of the interview process. It was better, and safer, but that still doesn't mean I was ever good at it!

Once, during my part in the interview process for a new management position, I felt pretty sure that the female candidate was a good prospect. She had all the skill set and I thought she would probably fit in great with the other employees. As we chatted, I told her about casual Fridays. "We wear jeans and nice shirts, but no thongs," I explained.

Her eyes went large and she looked a bit confused, but said, "O...K...."

I blathered on about why it wasn't very businesslike to wear thongs, trying to understand her strange face, and again she gave me the big eyes and the slow, "O...K...."

My son happened to be walking by my office (the door was open, another safety move!) and he leaned in and said, "What dad means is no flip-flops or open-toed shoes are allowed."

After my reprimand, that was the last interview I ever did! And I have never complained.

CHAPTER SIXTEEN

PERFECT PRACTICE

It was Vince Lombardi who said, "Practice does not make perfect. Only perfect practice makes perfect."

How can you apply this principle to your current or prospective business?

That is a question worth considering.

Creatures of Habit

You and I both know from personal experience that forming good habits is much harder than making bad habits. It's so easy to make bad habits, but we really have to work on the good ones.

Why is that? Why is one so hard and the other so easy? I believe part of the answer is that we are creatures of habit.

A good example is that bowl of ice cream. If I have a bowl a few evenings in a row, suddenly I want ice cream every evening! The bad habit is literally formed in just a few days ... but if I were trying to set a good habit, such as drinking herbal tea or going for a walk in the evenings, it would take weeks for the habit to form.

That is just the way it is!

Use Habits to Your Advantage

I have found there to be a powerful secret when it comes to habits:

> *Force yourself to form the habit you want, then use it to your advantage.*

In business, we need to practice making good decisions each and every day. That forms the habits you want and need for the future.

If you are not in the habit of making decisions, then that is the first habit to form. Force yourself to address the issues and make that necessary decision.

Next, if making good decisions doesn't come easily to you, force yourself to get the counsel and input you need so you can make that good decision.

Both steps, even if they are a little scary, will give you the good habits that you want. You and your business will benefit as a result!

Perfecting Your Practice

Once you have developed the habit of using good decision-making techniques, you will be moving toward "perfect practice." That is where things really take off!

Here is another principle that will help you along the way:

> *The more often you make good decisions, the easier it will become.*

It saddens me to think of how many potentially good businessmen never make it simply because they have not practiced good decision-making. Do not let that be you!

If you need further assistance in your decision-making, there are books, seminars, and colleagues who can assist you. Using habits to your advantage may mean that you find out what you need and you go after it until you get it.

Never forget that all businesses follow the same fundamentals from start to finish, from organizational structure to value.

Above all, the most important habit for you to form and live by is this:

Run your own business ... don't let your staff, employees, clients, or business run your business.

You will be successful if you run your business because nobody else will ever understand what you do, much less know the blood, sweat, and tears or the happiness and disappointment that you put into your business to make it successful.

Success is an attitude, not an accident!

CHAPTER SEVENTEEN

DEALING WITH THE CHAIN STORE

If you have products that could be sold in chain stores … when is the right time to present your offer to the chain store system?

The more appropriate question might be, "Are you sure you want to?"

As your business grows, you will either think of the potential profits of chain store sales or someone will suggest it. When it comes to selling products through chain stores, consider this:

Be careful what you wish for!

From Small to BIG

In most cases, a small startup business is not going to be able to handle the demands that will be put on them by the big chain stores.

It begins innocently enough, with the chain stores saying they only want a small percentage of your business, such as a mere 10% ... but as volume starts going up as they introduce your product to more and more stores, suddenly you have a major cash flow problem!

Why? Because you don't have enough working capital. Your working capital is budgeted as part of your own plan, and all is fine there, but the big chain store requirements were never built into your pro forma.

Remember the importance of preserving your working capital?

This is the perfect example of what can happen as your business grows. However:

> *Too much business too fast can be as bad as no business growth at all!*

Trust me on this one! I have seen and even experienced this several times throughout my career.

Backing Up Is Hard to Do

If you have taken a boat to the lake, you know there is a certain knack required to back a trailer up without hurting someone or breaking something. Add another trailer to your trailer and try backing that up!

Similarly, if your business starts growing rapidly through chain store sales and you lack the necessary working capital, it is extremely hard to back that up. Trust me!

I have seen many startups not make it because they got what they wished for! Do not be one of those statistics.

What should you do?

What you want is to grow your business at a steady pace. I know that does not sound very glamorous, but here is the truth:

> *If you will use good business sense now, you will be happy and your business will be healthier in the long run.*

That sure beats being sorry in the long run and having to close your business because you ran out of working capital.

The Art of the Deal

Even if you do use good business sense and grow at a steady pace, you still need to limit the amount of business going to any one store chain.

Why? I have found that once a particular chain has a significant amount of your business, they usually become very demanding. Situations arise that you would have never expected:

- "Your prices are too high. You need to cut your prices."
- "You need to ship smaller amounts to us or package them differently."
- "If you are going to do business with us, you need to give us a discount if paid within 10 days."
- "Since our company lets our customers return items no questions asked, even without a receipt, we expect you to also accept all returns of your products if they don't sell."
- "Even though the payment terms are net 30 days, we won't pay for 90 days."

How would your business fare if your chain store rep called with the news?

Mind you, these examples are real situations. I know firsthand the businesses that have dealt with these issues, and in many cases these very issues were lethal to the small businesses.

I remember one situation where the chain was supposed to pay the business within the agreed-upon net 30-day terms. It was in the contract … but that didn't stop them from paying in 90 days. The businessman was struggling. The chain represented too much of his business and he didn't have the working capital to carry the 90-day terms.

Taking action, he contacted the big chain's accounting department to try and speed up payments. He reached a supervisor in the accounting department who said, "Mark on the invoices 'discount 1% net days' and that will get you paid within 10-15 days."

He was okay with the 1% discount if it meant his cash flow problems were solved. He was pleased ... until the big chain still paid him 90 days later *and* took off the additional 1% from his invoice! It took him countless phone calls to sort out the 1% discount issue, but in the end, his business simply couldn't handle the 90-day terms.

I repeat ... even if you do use good business sense and grow at a steady pace, you still need to limit the amount of business going to any one store chain.

Take it slow, really slow, so that your relationship with the big chain stores is a blessing and not a curse.

All of this goes back to making sure you implement and live by the fundamentals that you started with when you founded your business.

CHAPTER EIGHTEEN

BRANDING YOU

Branding is a necessity. No doubt you know the jingles that have been drilled into our subconscious minds:

- "Let's go places" (Toyota)
- "I'm lovin it" (McDonalds)
- "You can do it, we can help" (Home Depot)

The list goes on and on. Do these branding campaigns work? You bet they do! Branding helps in countless ways, from sales to recognition to acceptance to referrals, it all helps grow your business.

Branding Yourself

If you are going to be in business, you must brand yourself. Whether you have a service business or a manufacturing business, you need to find a way to create a brand for you and your company.

Many years ago, a friend of mine owned an interior plant maintenance company. He said he did his due diligence and determined there was in fact a need for his services. There was, however, a company in town that seemed to have most of the business in the entire city. They had all their employees wear green company shirts.

My friend's products and services were better than the competition, but he had no brand ... so he issued his employees the same green colored shirts of his competitor. Whether you call green shirts a brand, the results of piggy backing on the competitor's shirt color was amazing! People began calling to have him bid their jobs.

The bottom line for you is this:

> *How are you going to brand yourself and your company?*

At the end of the day, it all comes down to sales. I'm always thinking, "What's going to attract people to my product or services?"

That is an integral part of branding. It might not be based on taste or value or price or proximity or color. The Super Bowl commercials, for example, are not trying to convince you their products are cheaper or better. At that level, it's all about branding at the subconscious level, mixed with humor, fanfare, social media, and as much buzz as possible.

In your business, keep your branding wheels in motion, and never stop.

CONCLUSION

When it all comes down to it, it comes down to you. That is always the case and the constant reality of the entrepreneur:

The buck stops with me, always.

This is an incredibly good thing because you have the power to create, plan, and be incredibly successful. It rests with you.

Being an entrepreneur is quite often a very lonely job. No one seems to see it like you do, no one takes on the risks like you do, and you have no one else to blame but yourself. However, no one has the opportunity to reap the rewards like you do!

In my opinion, being an entrepreneur is the greatest job on earth! It doesn't matter what type of business you are in, business is business.

Armed with the bedrock principles we have discussed in this book, I look forward to hearing great things from you.

That is because good business is just that ... *good* business. Customers and clients are looking for those few businesses that will treat them right, meet their needs, and be around for the long haul ... and that is you!

I wish you the best toward your inevitable success!

—Randy R. Steele

ABOUT THE AUTHOR

Randy Steele was the managing partner of Compass Pointe Financial, a wealth management firm dedicated to helping clients with their financial planning needs. From insurance to investments, the Compass Pointe Financial team advisors help business owners, high-net-worth clients, and average families with their savings, investing, and retirement plans. Whether it is transferring a small business or family farm from one generation to another or helping an entrepreneur facilitate a startup company, the advisors and local estate attorneys and tax consultants help the process be tax efficient as possible. Their honesty and down-to-earth approach is what continues to attract clients to their door.

Being active in Rotary, helping start a local school foundation, being active in church, and having 7 grandchildren ... all of it has given him important insight. In 1997, Randy was awarded MVP for Lutheran Brotherhood (a financial service business for Lutherans) and received the Million Dollar Round Table (MDRT) Top of the Table Award. The MDRT award is the top $1/10^{th}$ of 1%, all based on production.

Randy is a lifelong entrepreneur and has had tremendous success in the financial service business, real estate, real estate appraising, greenhouse growing operations, and the mortgage industry. Through these experiences, the knowledge he has gained is invaluable to someone wanting to start a business or someone wanting to take their business to the next level.

Through the years, Randy has been involved in starting numerous successful businesses. He never felt it was in his best interest to have a partner. Success or failure was his. However, in 2002, after running the numbers, it became evident the financial service business was an industry that not only had a great potential but also met his goals of future succession planning. Randy felt since this was going to be a huge undertaking it would be best if he could find a partner he could trust. His son-in-law, Jason Scarcella, was just that man. Smart, honest, and genuine, Jason had the right ingredients. Together, they co-founded Compass Pointe Financial.

To learn more, go to:

www.RandySteeleBooks.com

NOTES

NOTES

The Entrepreneur's
Roadmap to Success
—for building a successful business

Randy R. Steele

The Entrepreneur's Roadmap to Success
—for building a successful business

Published by Yorkshire Publishing
6271 E. 120ᵗʰ Court Suite 200 Tulsa, OK   74137
www.yorkshirepublishing.com

978-1-942451-32-7 - Standard Edition
978-1-942451-33-4 - eBook Edition
978-1-942451-43-3 - Special Financial Advisor Edition

Printed in the United States of America